FROM SEA to SHINING SEA

SOUTH DAKOTA

CARYN YACOWITZ

Consultants

MELISSA N. MATUSEVICH, PH.D.

Curriculum and Instruction Specialist
Blacksburg, Virginia

PAM CHAMBERLAIN

Children's Services Coordinator
South Dakota State Library

CHILDREN'S PRESS®

A DIVISION OF SCHOLASTIC INC.

New York • Toronto • London • Auckland • Sydney • Mexico City
New Delhi • Hong Kong • Danbury, Connecticut

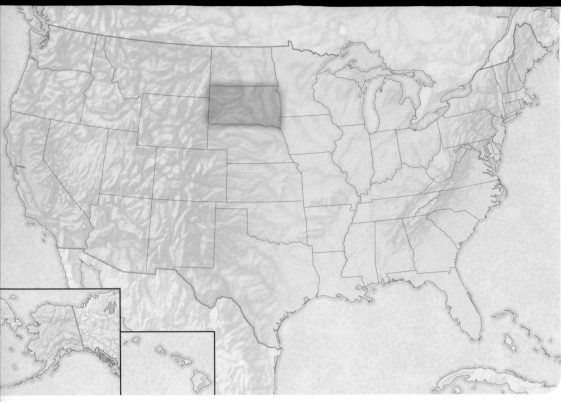

South Dakota is in the north central part of the United States. It is bordered by North Dakota, Minnesota, Iowa, Nebraska, Wyoming, and Montana.

The photograph on the front cover shows Mount Rushmore.

Project Editor: Meredith DeSousa
Art Director: Marie O'Neill
Photo Researcher: Marybeth Kavanagh
Design: Robin West, Ox and Company, Inc.
Page 6 map and recipe art: Susan Hunt Yule
All other maps: XNR Productions, Inc.

Library of Congress Cataloging-in-Publication Data

Yacowitz, Caryn.
        South Dakota / Caryn Yacowitz.
            p. cm. — (From sea to shining sea)
Includes bibliographical references (p.) and index.
Contents: Introducing South Dakota—The land of South Dakota—South Dakota through
history—Governing South Dakota—The people and places of South Dakota—South
Dakota almanac—Timeline—Gallery of famous South Dakotans—Glossary.
  ISBN 0-516-22394-1
  1. South Dakota—Juvenile literature. [1. South Dakota.] I. Title. II. Series.

F651.3.Y33 2003
978.3—dc21   2003004564

TABLE of CONTENTS

CHAPTER ONE

INTRODUCING THE MOUNT RUSHMORE STATE

South Dakota is blessed with many lakes, rich prairies, and beautiful scenery. Split Rock Creek at Palisades State Park is shown above.

South **Dakota has more nicknames than any other state.** Some of the nicknames, like the Sunshine State and the Blizzard State, come from the types of weather in South Dakota. Other nicknames are the Coyote State, for the state animal, and the Land of Infinite Variety, in reference to the great variety of climate and natural wonders within the state. South Dakota's official nickname is the Mount Rushmore State, after the most famous place in South Dakota. It is at Mount Rushmore that huge likenesses of four United States presidents are carved into the granite rock of the Black Hills.

South Dakota gets its name from the Native American tribes of the area. *Dakota* means "friends" or "allies" in the Lakota language. The Lakota and Dakota were the most powerful tribes when European settlers first came to this land of rolling, grass-covered prairies and mighty herds of buffalo. The mysterious Badlands and beautiful Black Hills, which are sacred to the Lakota, are also part of South Dakota.

Today, South Dakotans are known for being hardworking, honest, and friendly. Some live in cities such as Sioux Falls or Rapid City. Others live in small towns that dot the state. Many are farmers or ranchers, making South Dakota one of the most important agricultural states. There are seven times as many cattle, pigs, and sheep in South Dakota as there are people!

Even if you've never been to South Dakota, you may know about some of its famous people. Television newscaster Tom Brokaw and baseball manager Sparky Anderson are from South Dakota. So is well-known author Laura Ingalls Wilder, who wrote about growing up on the prairie. The stories in some of her *Little House* books really happened in South Dakota.

What else comes to mind when you think of South Dakota?
- Great herds of buffalo grazing on the plains
- The sculpture of Chief Crazy Horse pointing to the Black Hills
- Sunset in the mysterious Badlands
- Visitors exploring Jewel Cave National Monument
- Flower-covered prairies under a brilliant blue sky
- The wide, muddy Missouri River

South Dakota has a rich past and a bright future. To find out more about this special state, simply turn the page. Welcome to South Dakota!

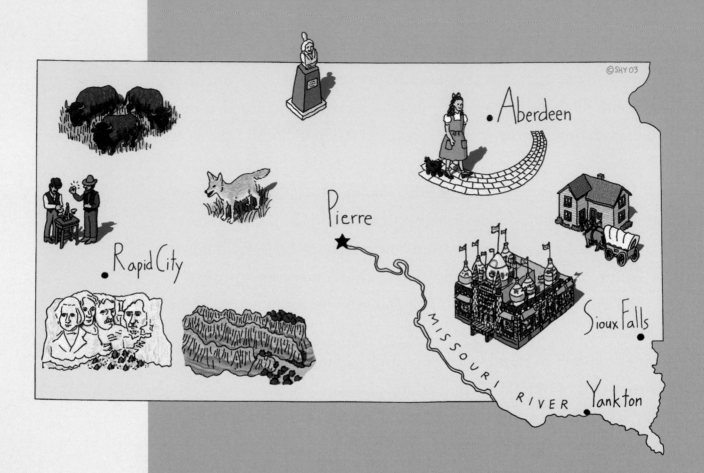

Aberdeen

Pierre

Rapid City

Sioux Falls

MISSOURI RIVER

Yankton

©SHY 03

CHAPTER TWO

THE LAND OF SOUTH DAKOTA

South Dakota is located in the Midwest, in the heart of the United States. It is surrounded by six other states—North Dakota to the north, Minnesota and Iowa to the east, Nebraska to the south, and Wyoming and Montana to the west. It is the seventeenth largest state, covering 77,122 square miles (199,745 square kilometers).

To draw a simple map of South Dakota, make a rectangle and take a bite out of the northeast corner. Then put a small "foot" or triangular "toe" on the lower-right corner. Now, draw a line down the middle, from top to bottom, pulling your pencil a little toward the "foot." You've drawn the Missouri River, one of the most important rivers in the United States. The Missouri River enters the state from North Dakota and flows south, dividing South Dakota almost in half. It leaves South Dakota at the southeast corner.

Spectacular granite rock formations line the edge of Sylvan Lake.

South Dakota is divided into four land regions. They are the Central Lowlands, the Missouri Hills, the Great Plains, and the Black Hills. Each region has its own special characteristics.

CENTRAL LOWLANDS

Most people in South Dakota live east of the Missouri River in an area of low, gently rolling prairies known as the Central Lowlands. The Central Lowlands cover the eastern third of the state. Stretching from east of the James River to South Dakota's border with Minnesota and Iowa, the Central Lowlands has fertile, loamy soil. It is known as Houdek soil. The rich, deep soil developed from rocks and other materials left by glaciers,

Crops flourish in the rich soil east of the Missouri River.

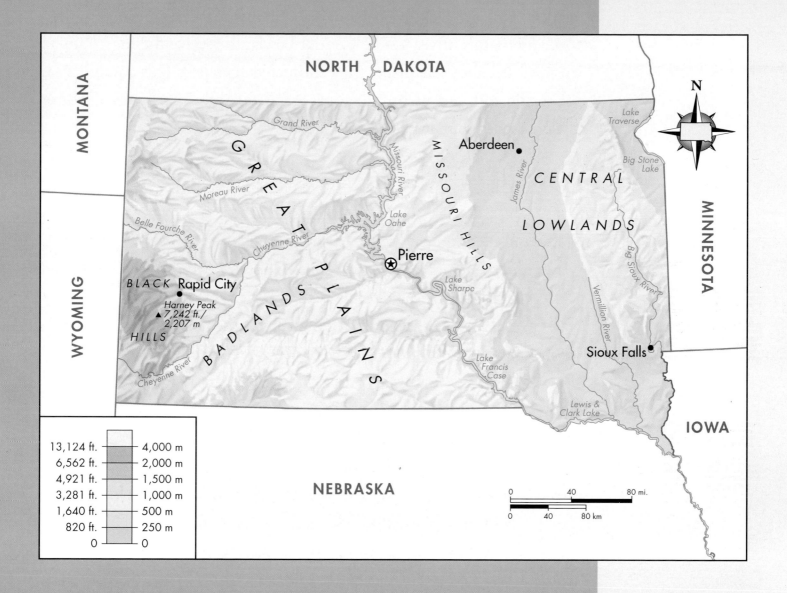

MONTANA

WYOMING

NORTH DAKOTA

MINNESOTA

IOWA

NEBRASKA

Grand River

Moreau River

Belle Fourche River

Cheyenne River

Cheyenne River

G R E A T

B A D L A N D S

P L A I N S

BLACK Rapid City

Harney Peak
▲ 7,242 ft./
2,207 m

HILLS

Missouri River

Lake Oahe

Pierre ✪

Lake Sharpe

Lake Francis Case

Lewis & Clark Lake

MISSOURI HILLS

James River

Aberdeen ●

CENTRAL

LOWLANDS

Lake Traverse

Big Stone Lake

Big Sioux River

Vermillion River

Sioux Falls ●

N

13,124 ft. — 4,000 m
6,562 ft. — 2,000 m
4,921 ft. — 1,500 m
3,281 ft. — 1,000 m
1,640 ft. — 500 m
820 ft. — 250 m
0 — 0

0   40   80 mi.

0   40   80 km

or thick sheets of ice, that covered the land long ago. The surface soil is dark brown or black from the decayed plants that have been deposited over thousands of years. The Central Lowlands receive the most rainfall in the state, about 22 inches (56 centimeters) per year. This combination of fertile soil and plentiful rain is good for farming. Most of South Dakota's farms are in this region.

MISSOURI HILLS

The land area known as the Missouri Hills lies between the Missouri River and the James River Basin. Glaciers also formed the rolling hills and valleys of this region. The soil is rich, but the area receives less rain than the Central Lowlands. Farmers and ranchers raise beef cattle and sheep in this region and grow crops such as barley, wheat, sunflowers, and hay.

GREAT PLAINS

The Great Plains are a large expanse of mostly flat, dry grasslands that stretch across a large area of west central North America, between the Rocky Mountains and the Mississippi River. In South Dakota the Great Plains cover almost two thirds of the state from west of the Missouri River to its borders with Montana and Wyoming. Coyotes, pronghorn deer, and prairie dogs live in these lands, where millions of buffalo once roamed. Today, cattle and sheep graze there.

(opposite)
Pastel-colored hills and cliffs are characteristic of the Badlands.

The Badlands are part of the Great Plains. Over thousands of years, water and wind have worn away, or eroded, the sandstone in this area. Strangely shaped rock formations, with soft-colored stripes of red, pink, yellow, and green, are seen there. The Lakota Tribe gave these lands their name, calling them *mako sica,* meaning "bad land." The Badlands are full of fossils, which are the hardened remains of plants and animals that lived millions of years ago.

Even though it looks dry and empty from a distance, thousands of animals live in the Badlands. Prairie dogs, bobcats, coyotes, foxes, jackrabbits, and badgers make it their home. There are also snakes and a variety of birds, including golden eagles. Six hundred buffalo live there as well.

Known as "the Needles," these granite spires in the Black Hills are popular with rock climbers.

BLACK HILLS

Contrasting with the Badlands are the Black Hills, located in the southwestern part of the state and stretching into eastern Wyoming. The Lakota called them *paha sapa,* meaning "hills of black." However, the Black Hills are not really black and they are not hills. Their lower

Bighorn sheep generally live near alpine meadows, grassy mountain slopes, and the foothills of rocky cliffs and bluffs.

slopes are covered with dense green forests of pine trees that make them *look* black from a distance. They are really coned mountains reaching more than 0.5 miles (0.8 km) high. The Black Hills were formed sixty million years ago, when dinosaurs began to disappear from Earth. They are rich in minerals, including gold, silver, copper, and lead.

Although most of South Dakota has very few trees, the Black Hills are the exception. Spruce, aspen, ponderosa pine, maple, ash, and willow trees grow there in abundance. Because of the rich vegetation and many streams, a great variety of animals live there. Elk, deer, mountain lions, bighorn sheep, Rocky Mountain goats, beavers, raccoons, muskrats, minks, wild turkeys, and porcupines are found in the Black Hills.

Visitors to the top of Harney Peak are welcomed by a stone tower, which once served as a fire observation site.

Harney Peak is the highest mountain in the Black Hills. It stands 7,242 feet (2,207 meters) high and is the highest place in the United States east of the Rocky Mountains. Harney Peak is also the highest peak between the Rockies and the Swiss Alps in Europe.

The Black Hills are sacred to the Lakota and Cheyenne Indians. Bear Butte, near the town of Sturgis, is the most sacred place in the Black Hills. Native Americans come to Bear Butte to fast and pray. For them, it is a place to be close to *Wankan Tanka,* the Great Spirit.

A railroad bridge spans the Missouri River.

RIVERS AND LAKES

The Missouri River is South Dakota's biggest and most important river. It begins near Three Forks, Montana, in the Rocky Mountains and flows southeast through South Dakota. At St. Louis, Missouri, it empties into the Mississippi River. The Missouri drains one-sixth of the land area of the United States and is famous for being muddy. Large amounts of sediment, which are tiny pieces of soil and sand, give it a muddy appearance. Farmers have described the river as "too thick to drink and too thin to plow."

Long ago the river often changed course and flooded large areas. In order to control flooding and to generate hydroelectric power (electricity that is produced by water power) for South Dakota, dams were built across the Missouri River in the 1950s and 1960s. These dams created four man-made lakes called the "Great Lakes of South Dakota." Lake Oahe is the largest. It covers almost 600 square miles (17,400 sq km). Lake Francis Case, Lake Sharpe, and Lewis and Clark Lake are the other "Great Lakes." The lakes are used for fishing, boating, and other recreation. Other rivers in South Dakota include the Big Sioux, Vermillion, and James rivers in the eastern part of the state and the Grand, Moreau, Cheyenne, and White rivers in the west.

In addition to the huge man-made lakes along the Missouri River, there are more than 300 natural lakes that were formed by glaciers. The largest natural lakes are in eastern South Dakota, including Lake Thompson, Lake Traverse, and Big Stone Lake. (Lake Traverse and Big Stone Lake are natural lakes that have been made larger by dams.)

SNOW, SUN, AND WIND

Two of South Dakota's nicknames have to do with the climate—the Sunshine State and the Blizzard State. South Dakota has one of the most extreme climates in the world. It gets very hot in summer, when skies are usually clear and bright. Most years, summer temperatures are between 80° and 90° Fahrenheit (27° and 32° Celsius).

In contrast, winters are very cold. Blizzards are common in South Dakota. Blizzards are windblown storms of snow and ice. South Dakota gets lots of snow, especially in February and March, when the state is usually under a thick white blanket of cold. Winter temperatures sometimes drop to 0° F (–18° C). The northeastern part of the state gets the coldest, with temperatures averaging –10° F (–23° C).

Eastern South Dakota gets the most precipitation, which is the moisture from both rain and melted snow. It receives 25 inches (51 cm) per year of precipitation. The northwest receives about 13 inches (33 cm),

Most South Dakotans are used to severe winter weather.

making it the driest area in the state. Droughts, or long periods during which no rain falls, sometimes occur in South Dakota.

In addition to temperature extremes, South Dakota has plenty of wind. The prairie wind blows steady just about all the time, causing old barns to lean over from the force of it. However, the constant wind of the prairie is tame compared with certain howling winds that sweep through the Black Hills.

In winter, dry, warm winds called chinooks descend from the eastern slopes of the Rocky Mountains into the Black Hills. Chinooks are formed when moist air moves in from the Pacific Ocean and condenses, dumping heavy rain on the western slopes of the Rocky Mountains. The warm, dry air travels over the Rockies, becoming even warmer and turning into winds speeding at 40 to 60 miles per hour (64 to 97 kilometers per hour). As the chinook races through the Black Hills, it causes temperatures to change very quickly. Native Americans call these fast winds "snow eaters."

Thanks to a chinook, the town of Spearfish recorded the greatest temperature change in United States history on January 22, 1943. In less than two minutes, the temperature rose from –4° F (–20° C) to 45° F (7° C). Glass windows cracked. Cattle were seen slipping and sliding in mud when moments before they had been standing on hard, frozen ground. Usually, chinooks melt snow and ice—up to 1 foot (0.3 m) per hour—and can make a winter day in the Black Hills suddenly feel like spring.

FIND OUT MORE

Wind can be used as a source of power. Find out how wind can be used to generate electricity. Is wind power used today in South Dakota?

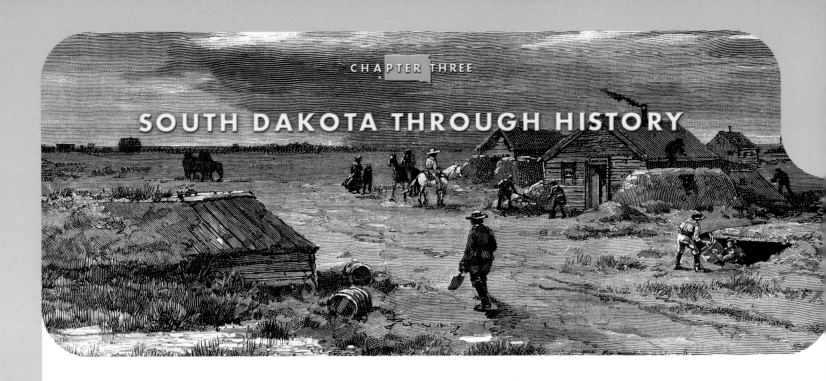

SOUTH DAKOTA THROUGH HISTORY

The earliest people in South Dakota were Paleo-Indians, who arrived more than 10,000 years ago. *Paleo* means "prehistoric" or "ancient." Paleo-Indians were hunters who followed game animals from place to place. They hunted enormous mammoths and giant bison. Over hundreds of years, the climate became drier and the huge mammals died off. The Paleo-Indians became hunter-gatherers, collecting berries, fruits, and roots; fishing; and hunting buffalo and smaller mammals.

About 2,000 years ago, people known as Plains Villagers settled in South Dakota. They were hunter-gardeners who lived in earth lodges near rivers. The Plains Villagers grew maize, which is a type of corn, and made pottery. Several hundred years ago, other bands moved into the area, replacing the early Plains Villagers. They were the Arikara and

Settlers in the Dakota Territory prepare for winter on the prairie.

19

Cheyenne. The Arikara lived along the Missouri River and farmed the fertile land, growing beans, corn, pumpkins, and squash. Like the earliest Plains Villagers, they lived in earth lodges.

The Cheyenne settled in the Black Hills. They hunted buffalo. Because they followed the buffalo herds, they needed houses that were portable, meaning they could take them apart and move them easily. Their buffalo skin tents, called tepees, could be packed up in minutes.

The bands that became the most powerful in the Great Plains came to South Dakota in the early 1700s. They were part of the Great Sioux Nation and included the Lakota, Dakota, and Nakota peoples. The Chippewa had pushed them out of Minnesota and Wisconsin. When the Sioux came to the Great Plains, they had to change their way of life. Instead of hunting small game and gathering roots and berries, they hunted buffalo.

They hunted on foot and later on horseback, using bows and arrows and spears. The Sioux depended on the buffalo for everything they needed. Their main food was buffalo meat, which they roasted or made into jerky by smoking strips of meat over a fire or drying them in the sun. Their clothing, bedding, and tepees were made from buffalo hides. Buffalo stomachs became water jugs. Buffalo tails became fly swatters. They made tools, utensils, and toys from the bones and horns and used buffalo manure ("buffalo chips") for fuel. They wasted nothing. John

The Great Sioux Nation once dominated the plains of South Dakota.

Lame Deer summed up the relationship of the Sioux with the buffalo when he said, "Everything we needed for life came from the buffalo's body. It was hard to say where the animal ended and the man began."

The Sioux ruled the Great Plains for more than one hundred years. They were excellent horsemen, daring hunters, and brave warriors. However, newcomers to the Great Plains would soon threaten their way of life.

FUR TRADERS AND EXPLORERS

The first Europeans to set foot in South Dakota were two French-Canadian brothers, François and Louis-Joseph de La Verendrye. They claimed the area for France. To prove they had been there, in 1743 they buried a 7-by-8-inch lead plate near what is now Fort Pierre. The plate stated that King Louis XV of France was the ruler of the land.

Native Americans were skilled trappers, and exchanged many furs for European goods.

The plate remained buried until 1913, when it was discovered by a group of high school students.

Soon, small numbers of French fur traders came to the area, seeking precious beaver and mink pelts, or skins. Traders could make money by sending the furs back to Europe, where they were sold and made into fancy hats and clothing. The Lakota, who were skilled hunters, traded furs and animal skins in exchange for European goods, such as pots and pans. Trade and relations between the Europeans and Native Americans was friendly. In the late 1700s, Pierre Dorion, a French fur trader, became the first European to permanently settle in South Dakota. He married a Dakota Sioux woman and lived near what is now the city of Yankton.

After a brief period in which Spain had control of the territory, France was once again the owner of the land that is now South Dakota, plus all the land west of the Mississippi River to the Rocky Mountains. This huge area was called the Louisiana Territory, named for the French king, Louis XIV. In 1803, the United States offered to buy the Louisiana Territory for 3 cents per acre. The French agreed. The United States paid France a total of $15 million in what became known as the Louisiana Purchase.

The United States struck a good deal. The Louisiana Purchase added more than 800,000 square miles (2 million sq km) to the United States. Later, South Dakota and all or part of fourteen other states would be carved out of this enormous territory.

LEWIS AND CLARK

After the United States bought the Louisiana Territory, people were curious to know what it was like. They also wanted to know if there was a good river route through the area to the Pacific Ocean. President Thomas Jefferson sent two men to explore the territory: Jefferson's personal secretary, Meriwether Lewis, and Lewis' friend, William Clark. The group they led was called the Corps of Discovery.

They began their journey in 1804 at the mouth of the Missouri River. It would take them two years to travel all the way to the Pacific Ocean and back. They traveled through South Dakota in 1804, coming up the Missouri River. Part of Lewis and Clark's job was to map the region and to keep careful diaries. They recorded information about the Native Americans they met and described plants, animals, birds, and rivers. Pierre Dorion, who had come to South Dakota many years before as the first white settler, became the group's Dakota Sioux language interpreter. A fifteen-year-old Indian girl named Sacagawea also

Sacagawea proved to be a valuable member of Lewis and Clark's expedition.

joined their Corps of Discovery and served as an interpreter and guide. When Lewis and Clark arrived home in Washington, D.C., they told everyone about the abundance of fur-bearing animals in South Dakota and other parts of the new territory. Soon, large numbers of fur traders and trappers traveled to the area.

The first permanent European settlement was a trading post near the center of present-day South Dakota. It was started by Joseph La Framboise in 1817 to establish a place where Europeans and Native Americans could come to trade goods with one another. The trading post later became Fort Tecumseh, then Fort Pierre.

This painting by Karl Bodmer shows a view of Fort Pierre in the early 1800s.

In the early to mid-1800s, as more traders and trappers came, fighting sometimes broke out between the newcomers and the Native Americans. The huge buffalo herds and other game that the Lakota and other bands depended on for food and shelter were being frightened away or killed by the settlers. The Native Americans' way of life was being threatened, and they fought to protect it. The fur frenzy lasted from about 1800 to 1850, when most of the fur-bearing animals were gone.

HOMESTEADERS

Following in the footsteps of the early trappers and traders were people who came for land. Some came from the eastern United States; others came from Europe. They wanted to settle in South Dakota and turn the prairie into farms and towns. In the 1860s, they came by the hundreds to homestead, which means to settle on the land and farm it. These early homesteaders settled in southeastern South Dakota, in Sioux Falls, Yankton, and Vermillion. This was land the United States government had purchased from the Lakota in the 1820s.

In 1861, Dakota Territory was created. The territory was carved out of the huge area bought in the Louisiana Purchase. The following year,

Because there were no trees or stones nearby, sod was the only material available for building homes.

the United States government passed the Homestead Act. This law offered settlers 160 acres (65 hectares) of land for free if they could "prove up." To prove up meant that settlers had to build a house on the land and live there for at least five years.

Proving up was difficult. There were no trees for wood. Some settlers lived in "dugouts," which were cavelike holes cut into the sides of hills. Most homesteaders used the earth of the prairie to build sod houses. Soddies were made of earth strips cut from the ground and stacked like bricks. The soddies were cool in summer and warm in winter. They were sturdy and didn't fall over in the constant prairie wind.

Families struggled to plant corn and wheat in soil that was a tangle of prairie grass roots. They were lucky if there was enough rain and their crops grew. Often, prairie fires, droughts, and huge clouds of grasshoppers destroyed everything they planted. They faced freezing blizzards and the loneliness of living in a sea of unending grass, with the nearest neighbor many miles away. Only four in every ten homesteaders managed to prove up.

As hard as life was on the prairie, settlers continued to come. By 1870, almost 12,000 people were homesteading. The first railroad was built in 1873 from Iowa to the new towns of Vermillion and Yankton.

Soon, even more land-hungry people arrived. Newspaper advertisements claimed that the best farming and grazing land in the world was in South Dakota. Two railroad companies began laying tracks between the small towns. The Chicago, Milwaukee & Saint Paul Railroad was called the Milwaukee Road. The other was the Chicago & North Western Railroad, or the C&NW. The trains brought people, food, fuel, tools, and other supplies. New immigrants came from Germany, Austria,

In 1888, people lined the streets of Deadwood to celebrate the completion of a section of railroad.

Hundreds of thousands of buffalo were shot for sport in the mid-1800s.

Norway, Sweden, Russia, Denmark, and Holland.

South Dakota was changing in other ways too. During these years, great herds of buffalo were slaughtered. Many were killed for their hides, which brought three dollars each in the east. That was a week's wages for most workers in the United States. Millions more buffalo were killed and left to rot on the prairie. The United States government encouraged the slaughter of buffalo because officials believed that destroying the buffalo would defeat the Native Americans. In the years between 1800 and 1900, as many as sixty million buffalo were killed on the Great Plains. By 1900, only a few hundred were left alive.

By the 1850s and 1860s, when hundreds of thousands of settlers came, it was difficult for the Lakota and other bands to defend their land and their way of life. The settlers looked down on Native Americans and thought of them as savages. The settlers also believed that the Native Americans did not have any right to the land. As a result of these conflicts, there were many battles between the Sioux and the United States Army, who were sent to protect the settlers of South Dakota.

Lakota leaders were often forced to sign treaties, or agreements, with the United States government just to protect small sections of their land. In 1851, Native American leaders signed an agreement known as the Fort Laramie Treaty. Sixty million acres (24 million ha) were assigned to the Lakota Nation. Later, Chief Red Cloud signed the Fort Laramie Treaty of 1868, which established the Great Sioux Reservation. It included the sacred Black Hills and all the land stretching from the Missouri River to the Bighorn Mountains. This treaty stated that "No white person or persons shall be permitted to settle upon or occupy any portion of the territory, or without consent of the Indians, to pass through . . ." The treaty also said that the United States Army would protect the Lakota against white settlement in the Black Hills.

THE GOLD RUSH

If the promise of free land brought people to South Dakota, it was nothing compared to the gold rush. The first hint that there was gold in South Dakota came in 1848 when Father Pierre-Jean De Smet visited the Black Hills. A Lakota chief showed him a bag of shiny gold dust. De Smet knew that people went crazy for gold, and he told the chief to keep it a secret. "Put it away and show it to nobody," De Smet warned.

WHO'S WHO IN SOUTH DAKOTA?

Crazy Horse (c. 1842–1877) was a Lakota chief and a fierce warrior. He committed his life to preserving the values and traditions of his people. He helped defeat Lieutenant Colonel Custer at the Battle of the Little Bighorn in Montana and fought to protect the sacred Black Hills. The legendary chief was never photographed; the painting at right is a rendering by artist Robert Ottokar Lindneux.

If the gold had been kept secret, the Lakota might have been left in peace in their beautiful, sacred *paha sapa*. However, the secret got out when Lieutenant Colonel George Armstrong Custer was sent to the Black Hills in 1874 to gather information. When he wrote that gold was everywhere in the Black Hills, Chicago newspapers announced it to the world. The stampede for gold was on.

Thousands of gold seekers poured into the Black Hills. The towns of Custer, Lead, and Deadwood sprang up. Deadwood was rough, dirty, and crowded—a true Wild West town. Outlaws roamed the area and guns, not laws, settled arguments. Frontierswoman Calamity Jane lived there for a while. So did James Butler Hickok, who was better known

Deadwood was born during the gold rush of 1876.

as the sharpshooter and frontier marshal Wild Bill Hickok.

Once the gold rush began, the government would no longer honor the terms of the Fort Laramie Treaty of 1868, refusing to keep miners out of the Black Hills. Instead, the government tried to force the Lakota to sell *paha sapa*. The Lakota refused. "I want you to go and tell the Great Father that I do not want to sell any land to the government," Chief Sitting Bull said. Then he bent and picked up a tiny speck of dust. "Not even as much as this."

To force the Lakota out, the government used a "sell or starve" policy. The food the government had promised to deliver to the reservations was much less than what was agreed upon. In 1889, the government forced the Lakota to give up almost half of the Great Sioux Reservation. It was divided into six smaller reservations and was later reduced even more.

Each time the government took land from Native Americans, they offered it to settlers. Thousands of immigrants poured into South Dakota in one of the last huge land rushes in United States history. Between 1870 and 1880, the population of South Dakota increased from 10,000 to 82,000. It was called the "Great Dakota Boom."

There were many battles between the United States Army and the Native Americans during these years. Under the leadership of Chief

Sitting Bull, Gall, and Crazy Horse, the Lakota tried to defend their lands. The pressure from so many settlers and gold seekers, who were protected by the United States Army, forced the tribes of South Dakota to give up their land and lifestyle on the open plains.

The hardest blow came on December 29, 1890, when more than three hundred Lakota were massacred at Wounded Knee Creek on the Pine Ridge Reservation. The army had been sent to arrest Chief Big Foot and disarm his warriors, but confusion and fear on both sides led to the massacre. Old people, women, and children were killed, as was their leader, Chief Big Foot.

Black Elk was a thirteen-year-old Lakota boy who survived. Years later he said, "I did not know then how much was ended. When I look back now from this high hill of my old age, I can still see all the women and children lying and scattered . . . And I can see that something else died there in the bloody mud, and was buried in the blizzard. A people's dream died there. It was a beautiful dream . . ."

The massacre at Wounded Knee broke the spirit of the Lakota and other bands. It ended Native American resistance. It would take almost eighty years for the Native American spirit to begin to grow strong again.

STATEHOOD

There were about 330,000 people living in the Dakota Territory by 1890. However, people living in territories did not have all the rights enjoyed by people living in states. They could not vote for their leaders. Instead, a territorial governor was appointed by the president of the United States. They also could not elect representatives to the United States Congress to help create laws for the country. People in the Dakota Territory wanted the region to become a state so they could have these rights. However, everyone had different ideas about how the territory should be divided.

The answer became clear in 1883, when territorial governor Nehemiah Ordway moved the capital from Yankton in the south to Bismarck in the north. People were angry because most of the population lived near Yankton. People in the southern part of the Dakota Territory decided they wanted two states: South Dakota and North Dakota. Finally, in 1889, Congress passed the Omnibus State Bill. The bill declared statehood for South Dakota and North Dakota.

No one knows for sure whether North Dakota or South Dakota became a state first. On November 2, 1889, President Benjamin Harrison intentionally shuffled the papers before he signed them. However, South Dakota considers itself the fortieth state because its twin sister,

Although Pierre was a temporary capital at the time of statehood, it was soon voted the permanent capital city by South Dakotans.

North Dakota, comes first alphabetically. The small town of Pierre was chosen as the capital because it was in the center of the new state.

FAMOUS FIRSTS

- The first photograph showing the curvature of Earth was taken from a balloon launched from Rapid City.
- The first monument to a Native American is the Crazy Horse Monument.
- The first Native American Day was celebrated in South Dakota on October 8, 1990.

HARD TIMES

The years following statehood were very hard for homesteaders. Droughts and severe blizzards drove some people out. Diseases such as cholera, pneumonia, and tuberculosis left many dead. This period was known as the "Great Dakota Bust." Many people left the state in search of a better life elsewhere.

Still, many homesteaders were determined to make it. Most were married couples. Twelve of every hundred were single women. Sometimes sisters would work together to prove up. The homesteaders were among the most hardworking people ever to settle in South Dakota.

Things began to change when World War I (1914–1918) broke out in Europe. After the United States entered the war in 1917, many South Dakotans served in the armed forces and fought overseas. At home, South Dakota farmers and ranchers helped feed the troops by sending wheat, oats, and beef. Prices for farm goods and land were high during the war years. Farmers who had been able to hold onto their farms during the drought years were now doing well.

The prosperity of the war years was followed by more hard times. In the 1920s, prices for farm crops dropped. Wheat that had sold for two dollars a bushel during the war brought less than one dollar by 1920. In October 1929, the stock market crashed, and the entire country was thrown into the Great Depression (1929–1939). Banks failed, factories closed, and millions of people were out of work. Long lines formed at soup kitchens, where hungry people who could not afford to buy food could get something to eat for free.

To make matters worse, a drought began in 1930. Thick blankets of dust covered the dry fields, and crops and livestock died. Thousands of grasshoppers swarmed down to eat every blade of wheat, corn, and vegetable that had not withered in the scorching heat. Powerful winds lifted the parched, bare soil into the air. "Black blizzards" of topsoil darkened the daytime sky. Dust covered every surface inside homes.

Giant dust storms ruined crops and destroyed grazing land.

The "dust bowl" was caused by a combination of drought and poor farming practices. For thousands of years, before people began farming and raising livestock on the plains, wild grasses held the soil in place. During World War I, when the demand for wheat was great and new farm machinery was available, hundreds of thousands of acres of Great Plains grasslands were turned into wheat fields. The land was also stripped bare by the overgrazing of cattle and sheep herds. The dust bowl lasted for ten years. During that time, 50,000 people left South Dakota looking for other places to live.

Leaders of the United States government helped the people of South Dakota by creating jobs during these difficult years. People planted trees in the Black Hills. They built bridges and buildings. Farmers were shown how to plant wheat lands with grasses that held topsoil in place with their deep roots.

Just as the dust bowl years were ending, World War II (1939–1945) was beginning in Europe. Many countries of the world fought one another in this war, and millions of people died. The United States entered the war in 1941. South Dakota farmers broke production records to supply food for U.S. military troops, sending meat, wheat, and dairy products. More than 68,000 men and women from South Dakota served their country in the armed forces. A small group of Native Americans from South Dakota helped the United States win the war by using their Indian language as a secret code. They were called code talkers. The enemy was never able to break, or figure out, the code. The Lakota, Navajo, and Comanche code talkers came from various states in the West.

After the war, new types of farm machinery, such as reapers, automatic cow milking machines, balers and choppers, and combines, helped farmers produce more food. The machines were so efficient that fewer farmers were needed, putting many farmers out of work. Some

Many farmers gave up their farms and worked on projects for the government in the 1930s. These workers are building a bridge spillway near Pierre.

FIND OUT MORE

Throughout history, people have created secret codes to protect information they don't want to share. What are some of the types of codes people have used? Make up a simple code to send messages to friends. Try it to see if it works. Next, try to break someone else's code.

went to towns, searching for jobs. Many young people left South Dakota to look for work in other states.

Some people found work on one of the biggest building projects in South Dakota history. The Pick-Sloan Missouri Basin Program was a building project designed to provide electric power, irrigation, and flood control in the Missouri River basin. It included building four dams across the Missouri River in South Dakota (as well as one in North Dakota and one in Montana) to produce hydroelectric power, or electric power created from the force of flowing water. The building of four dams—Gavins Point, Big Bend, Oahe, and Fort Randall—also created four large lakes. They are called the Great Lakes of South Dakota because they are the largest lakes in the state, just as the Great Lakes in the Midwest and Northeast are the largest lakes in the United States. In addition to supplying electric power, the dams helped prevent flooding from the Missouri River and provided water for irrigation and recreation.

The Oahe Dam and power plant provides electricity for residents in parts of Nebraska, Minnesota, Montana, and North and South Dakota.

In the 1950s and 1960s, the tourist industry began to boom. Farmers and ranchers in South Dakota got good prices for meat, grain, and other products. Most people in South Dakota enjoyed a time of prosperity, meaning they were earning enough money to have the things they needed, such as good homes, food, education, and health care.

AMERICAN INDIAN MOVEMENT

Although many South Dakotans prospered during this time, Native Americans did not. The reservations of South Dakota were among the poorest places in the United States. The main reason for this poverty was a lack of jobs in and around the reservations. Only one in three adults could get work. Schools were in bad condition, and the few schoolbooks available were old. The main ingredient for education—good teachers—was also lacking. Poverty led to crime, despair, and broken spirits throughout the Native American community.

On February 27, 1973, a group of 200 Native Americans occupied the trading post and Catholic church in the village of Wounded Knee on the Pine Ridge Reservation. Some were armed members of the American Indian Movement (AIM), a civil rights group led by Russell Means and Dennis Banks. Others were traditional Oglala Lakotas. They demanded free elections of tribal leaders, better treatment of Native Americans, and a review of treaties between the federal government and native people, especially the Fort Laramie Treaty of 1868. They held Wounded Knee for 71 days. Finally, the U.S. government

WHO'S WHO IN SOUTH DAKOTA?

Peter Norbeck (1870–1936) was the first governor of South Dakota who was born there. He was elected to the U.S. Senate in 1920. Norbeck helped to establish Custer State Park in 1919 to encourage tourism in South Dakota. He also encouraged the building of scenic roads such as Needles Highway and Iron Mountain Road. Norbeck was born in southeastern Dakota Territory.

In 1973, Native Americans seized Wounded Knee, the site of the last official battle of the Indian Wars.

agreed to talk about the Fort Laramie Treaty and the Native Americans surrendered.

In 1979, the United States Court of Appeals declared that the federal government had broken the Fort Laramie Treaty of 1868. The Black Hills had been taken from the Lakota illegally. The Court's ruling stated that "A more ripe and rank case of dishonorable dealing will never, in all probability, be found in our history."

Most importantly, the Wounded Knee incident renewed the pride and spirit of Native Americans. It was the beginning of the modern American Indian movement. They became determined to be heard and to make their traditions and culture strong again.

Although the federal government offered to pay the Lakota $106 million for the Black Hills, they refused to accept the offer. The Lakota simply wanted their sacred places returned to them. The Lakota are still working to get *paha sapa* back.

Since 1988, the lives of some Native Americans in South Dakota have improved. That was the year gambling (playing games

The government has helped to build homes like these on the Pine Ridge Reservation in an effort to create strong communities and provide better housing for Native Americans.

for money) was first allowed on the reservations. Jobs were created in the gambling casinos, which attract millions of tourists. On October 8, 1990, the people of South Dakota celebrated the first Native American Day in the United States. It has replaced Columbus Day in South Dakota and is a way for all South Dakotans to honor the first Americans.

Farmers in South Dakota suffered through a terrible drought in 1988. The drought forced almost half the state's farmers to sell their farms. In 1990, about 35,000 farms remained, compared to 68,000 farms just ten years before. There were as many people living in cities and towns as on farms. By 1999, there were just 32,500 farms left. People in South Dakota were sad to see farms sold. As one farmer said, "I'd rather have my neighbor than his farm."

Although there are fewer farms in South Dakota, another industry has been growing quickly—tourism. Millions of people from the United States and around the world visit South Dakota each year. Tourists spent $1.25 billion there in 2000. Tourism creates jobs for thousands of South Dakotans at hotels, parks, and resorts.

People in South Dakota are optimistic about the future. They are ready to face problems and work together to solve them. They are proud of their state and want all its citizens to have jobs, healthcare, and a good education.

WHO'S WHO IN SOUTH DAKOTA?

Russell Means (1939–) is an American Indian rights activist and movie star. The *Los Angeles Times* called him the "most famous American Indian since Sitting Bull and Crazy Horse." He was a leader of the Wounded Knee occupation in 1973 and one of AIM's best-known spokespeople. He also starred in the film *The Last of the Mohicans*. Means was born on the Pine Ridge Indian Reservation.

CHAPTER FOUR

GOVERNING SOUTH DAKOTA

When **South Dakota became a state,** people wanted a system to create and enforce laws for South Dakotans, in addition to the federal laws that helped govern the country. The state's first constitution, or set of laws, was adopted in 1889, the same year South Dakota became a state. Over the years, it has been amended, or changed, more than eighty times. State laws govern many things that are important to the everyday lives of its citizens—roads and driver licenses; school standards and testing; and training for teachers, doctors, and nurses, among other things.

South Dakota's constitution divides the state government into three parts, or branches: the legislative, executive, and judicial branches. Each branch plays a special role. Each branch also serves as a "check" for the other branches so that no part of government becomes too powerful. Instead, each one checks and balances the power of the other.

South Dakota's state government centers around the capitol building in Pierre.

A group of students watches the state senate in action.

LEGISLATIVE BRANCH

The job of the legislative branch is to make laws. It also passes the budget, or plan for spending the state's money, so there will be funds to pay for things such as roads, schools, prisons, and parks. The legislative branch is bicameral, meaning it is divided into two parts, each with equal power. One group is the senate. The other is the house of representatives. The senate has thirty-five members, called senators. The house of representatives has seventy members, called representatives. People from both groups are sometimes referred to as legislators, meaning people who make laws.

The state is divided into different districts, or parts, so people can vote for legislators from their part of the state. Legislators want to know what people in their district need, such as better schools, and what problems they face. Usually, people are eager to discuss these issues with legislators.

Unlike many other states, South Dakota's senators and representatives are not professional politicians. They are teachers, lawyers, farmers, or businesspeople who come to the capital city of Pierre each winter to discuss new laws

EXTRA! EXTRA!

Citizens of South Dakota can suggest new laws without the help of their senator or representative. First, they must write down what they think the law should be. Then, they must find other people who agree with the proposed new law. If enough people are in favor of it, it becomes an initiative, meaning voters all over the state can vote to approve the proposed law during the next election.

and vote on them. Senators and representatives are elected for two-year terms. They may not serve more than four terms in a row, or eight years.

EXECUTIVE BRANCH

The executive branch is in charge of making sure the laws of the state are carried out. The governor, who is the head of the executive branch, is the highest-ranking elected official in the state. In addition to enforcing laws, the governor listens to what residents of the state want and makes sure they get help when disasters strike. He or she is also head of the National Guard and may ask for its help during natural disasters, such as floods, droughts, blizzards, and fires. Finally, the governor appoints high-ranking officials and creates special task forces to deal with important issues such as education or the environment.

The governor also plays a role in creating new laws. After a bill (a proposed new law) has received enough votes in the legislature, it goes to the governor. The governor must sign the bill before it can become a law. Sometimes the governor vetoes, or rejects, a bill.

The governor's mansion in Pierre has been home to many of South Dakota's governors and their families.

SOUTH DAKOTA GOVERNORS

Name	Term	Name	Term
Arthur C. Mellette	1889–1893	M. Q. Sharpe	1943–1947
Charles H. Sheldon	1893–1897	George T. Mickelson	1947–1951
Andrew E. Lee	1897–1901	Sigurd Anderson	1951–1955
Charles N. Herreid	1901–1905	Joseph J. Foss	1955–1959
Samuel H. Elrod	1905–1907	Ralph Herseth	1959–1961
Coe I. Crawford	1907–1909	Archie Gubbrud	1961–1965
Robert S. Vessey	1909–1913	Nils Boe	1965–1969
Frank M. Byrne	1913–1917	Frank L. Farrar	1969–1971
Peter Norbeck	1917–1921	Richard F. Kneip	1971–1978
W. H. McMaster	1921–1925	Harvey L. Wollman	1978–1979
Carl Gunderson	1925–1927	William J. Janklow	1979–1987
W. J. Bulow	1927–1931	George S. Mickelson	1987–1993
Warren Green	1931–1933	Walter D. Miller	1993–1995
Thomas Berry	1933–1937	William J. Janklow	1995–2003
Leslie Jensen	1937–1939	Mike Rounds	2003–
Harlan J. Bushfield	1939–1943		

SOUTH DAKOTA STATE GOVERNMENT

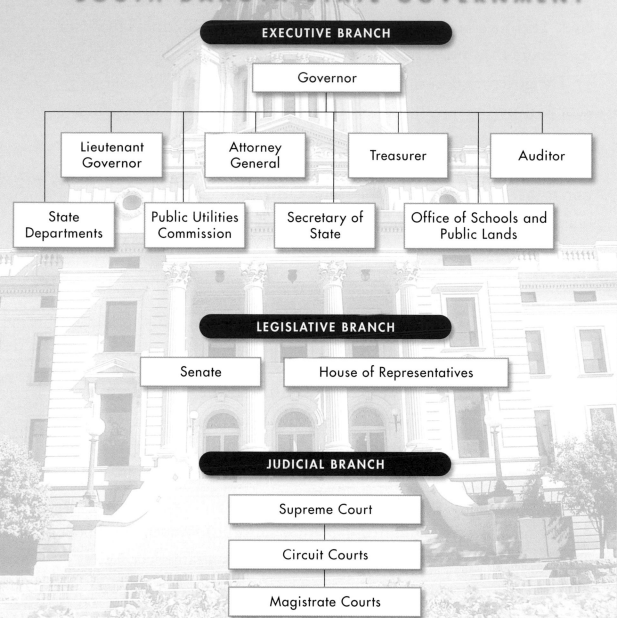

EXECUTIVE BRANCH

Governor

Lieutenant Governor

Attorney General

Treasurer

Auditor

State Departments

Public Utilities Commission

Secretary of State

Office of Schools and Public Lands

LEGISLATIVE BRANCH

Senate

House of Representatives

JUDICIAL BRANCH

Supreme Court

Circuit Courts

Magistrate Courts

When this happens, the bill goes back to the legislature to be reconsidered. The governor is elected to a four-year term. Governors may not serve more than two terms in a row, or eight years.

The governor does not work alone. People who head different agencies, or departments, such as education, transportation, and agriculture (farming), are appointed, or chosen, by the governor. This group is called the cabinet. Cabinet members work very closely with the governor to help the state run smoothly. Other officials in the executive branch include the lieutenant governor, attorney general, secretary of state, state treasurer, and state auditor.

JUDICIAL BRANCH

The job of the judicial branch is to settle arguments about the law and to decide punishments for people who break the law. The judicial branch includes all the courts in the state.

Many cases begin in circuit court. These are trial courts that handle civil and criminal cases. Civil cases settle disputes between two or more parties about property rights and personal rights. Criminal cases deal with crimes, or acts committed that are against the law, such as robbery. The state is divided into eight areas called circuits, or districts. Voters in each area elect circuit court judges to serve for a term of eight years.

The most powerful court in South Dakota is the state supreme court. The governor appoints five judges, called justices, to the supreme court. Together, they vote to choose a chief justice; the others are called associate justices. The supreme court decides whether laws uphold the state constitution. It also has the power to declare the actions of the governor unconstitutional, meaning the constitution does not permit those actions.

The supreme court is a court of appeal. This means that if people are not satisfied with a decision made in circuit court, they may request an appeal, or a review of the case, by the supreme court. For example, if someone is found guilty of a crime in a lower court, he or she may appeal the case in the supreme court. If the court finds that a mistake was made during the trial, then the decision of the lower court may be overturned.

South Dakota also has magistrate courts to handle small cases. Magistrate courts hear cases involving minor crimes, perform marriages, and settle small claims. There are magistrate courts in each district.

TAKE A TOUR OF PIERRE, THE STATE CAPITAL

The state capital of Pierre (pronounced "pier" by South Dakotans) is located in the center of South Dakota. It is small town with fewer than 15,000 people.

Pierre is a small town nestled along the Missouri River.

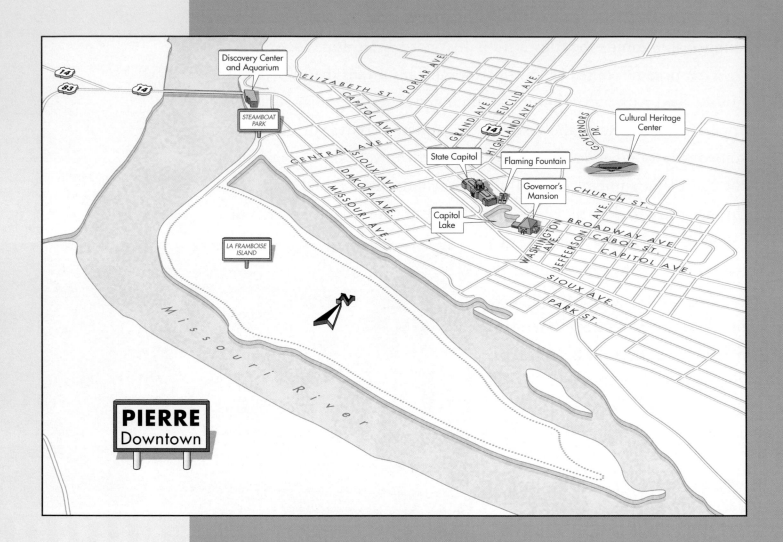

Discovery Center
and Aquarium

STEAMBOAT
PARK

ELIZABETH ST.

POPLAR AVE.

CAPITOL AVE.

GRAND AVE.

EUCLID AVE.

HIGHLAND AVE.

14

CENTRAL AVE.

SIOUX AVE.

DAKOTA AVE.

MISSOURI AVE.

GOVERNORS DR.

Cultural Heritage
Center

State Capitol

Flaming Fountain

Governor's
Mansion

CHURCH ST.

Capitol
Lake

LA FRAMBOISE
ISLAND

WASHINGTON AVE.

JEFFERSON AVE.

BROADWAY AVE.

CABOT ST.

CAPITOL AVE.

SIOUX AVE.

PARK ST.

Missouri River

PIERRE
Downtown

Pierre was appointed the interim (temporary) capital when South Dakota became a state in 1889. It became the permanent capital in 1904. Pierre campaigned so hard for the honor of being the capital that it was in debt for thirty years! South Dakotans are proud of their beautiful and friendly capital city. There are many things to see and do in and around Pierre.

The capitol building is one of the prettiest in the country. It was built in 1910 and restored for the state's one hundredth birthday in 1989. The building is made of Marquette sandstone and Indiana limestone, with a dome made of solid copper. On the capitol grounds stands the Fighting Stallions Memorial to Governor George Mickelson. Mickelson died in a plane crash in April 1993 along with seven others. The memorial is a replica of a sculpture by Korczak Ziolkowski, carver of the Crazy Horse Memorial. Inside the capitol, an interesting and unusual display is the First Lady Gown Collection. Doll-like figures wear reproductions of gowns worn by wives and sisters of South Dakota's governors when they celebrated taking office.

The South Dakota Cultural Heritage Center is also a must-see. It has displays about the history and culture of South Dakota. You can see a full-sized Lakota tepee, learn about South Dakota's railroads and riverboats, and touch a soft, thick buffalo robe. The famous Verendrye Plate is also on display there. The Verendrye brothers were the first Europeans to come to South Dakota. In 1743, they buried a small lead plate on a hill above the city. It says, "In the twenty-sixth year of the reign of Louis XV, the most illustrious Lord, the Lord Marquis of Beauharnois being

At the South Dakota Cultural Heritage Center, you can see Native American objects and walk through a sod house to learn more about the history of the state.

Viceroy, 1741, Peter Gaultier de La Verendrye placed this." The brothers claimed all the land of South Dakota for the king of France. The Verendrye Monument just outside Pierre marks the area where the plate was buried.

Nearby is Fort Pierre Chouteau. The American Fur Company built the fort in 1832 to replace the older trading post there. This was the largest fur trading post on the upper Missouri River. Native Americans traded 17,000 buffalo hides each year for pots, pans, ammunition, and other goods.

CHAPTER FIVE

THE PEOPLE AND PLACES OF SOUTH DAKOTA

According to the 2000 census, 754,844 people live in South Dakota. Of every 100 South Dakotans, 91 are of European descent, almost 8 are Native American, 1 is Hispanic (someone from Latin America living in the United States, especially someone from Mexico, Puerto Rico, or Cuba), and 1 is either African-American or Asian.

About half of South Dakotans live on farms or ranches, and the other half live in small towns or cities. Sioux Falls is the largest city in South Dakota. It has a population of 123,975. Rapid City is the next largest city, with a population of 59,607—about half that of Sioux Falls. Other cities in the state are much smaller, including Aberdeen, Watertown, Brookings, Mitchell, Pierre, Huron, and Vermillion.

Many towns have festivals celebrating the European heritage of their ancestors, the early settlers. They enjoy music, food, and dancing from Germany, Austria, Russia, Sweden, Holland, Finland, Denmark, the

Watching the rodeo is a popular pastime in South Dakota.

Czech Republic, and Norway. Sometimes they dress in colorful costumes from the "old country." Many people of German descent still live in the area of Sioux Falls and Aberdeen, where their ancestors settled. Many Czechs live in Tabor, and Scandinavians live in Canton, Sioux Falls, and Watertown.

Most Native Americans in South Dakota live on one of nine reservations or spend part of the year there. They return to the Pine Ridge, Standing Rock, Lower Brule, Crow Creek, Cheyenne River, Yankton, Flandreau Santee Sioux, Sisseton Wahpeton, and Rosebud Reservations, even if they work in a city, town, or ranch the rest of the year. The Lakota are working to preserve their culture, speak their language, and teach their

In February 2000, kuchen, a delicious German dessert, was declared the state dessert of South Dakota. More than half the people living in South Dakota today are descendants of German settlers. The family recipe below was brought to South Dakota from Germany more than 100 years ago by Hattie Tiede of Wessington Springs. Don't forget to ask an adult for help!

KUCHEN

Dough
1 cup warm water
1/2 tsp. sugar
1 package yeast
1/4 cup shortening
1 tsp. salt
2 small eggs
4 cups flour

Topping
1 cup apples, peaches, prunes, or apricots
1/2 cup cream
1/2 cup sugar
2 egg yolks
cinnamon and sugar

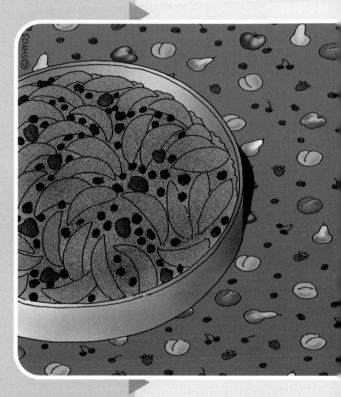

1. Soak yeast and sugar in 1/4 cup warm water in a small bowl.
2. In a larger bowl, mix 2 cups flour with 3/4 cup warm water and eggs.
3. Add yeast mixture, shortening, salt, and mix well. Add remainder of flour.
4. Knead mixture with hands until dough is soft and easy to handle (not sticky). Place in greased bowl and let rise (about 1 hour). Then punch down and let rise again (about 45 minutes).
5. Grease 2 pie pans with shortening. Shape dough into pans like a pie crust, but not as thin. Press dough up the sides of the pan. Let rise again.
6. After dough has risen, cut fruit into small pieces and punch into top of dough.
7. Beat egg yolks, add sugar and cream and cook until thickened.
8. Pour topping over fruit and dough. Sprinkle with cinnamon and sugar.
9. Bake 20 minutes at 350 to 375 degrees.

A young Native American prepares for a powwow.

children about their rich heritage. Powwows are held on reservations each year so that Native Americans and people of other cultures can enjoy traditional dancing, singing, and food. Powwows are an important link between tribal members and a way for different tribes to connect with one another.

WORKING IN SOUTH DAKOTA

Ranches and farms cover 9 in 10 acres (3.6 in 4 hectares) in the state. About half the workers in South Dakota have jobs in agriculture (farming). There are about 32,500 farms in South Dakota. Farmers produced more than nine million tons of hay in 2001, making South Dakota one of the nation's top producers of baled hay. Farmers also grow oats, sunflowers, rye, flaxseed, and corn. Ranchers raise almost four million cattle and calves. They also raise hogs, pigs, and sheep.

Many people who live in the cities and towns work in the service industry. For example, they might sell products in stores, work for the government, or provide services for visitors (tourism). Some South Dakotans also work in manufacturing, producing various products.

Some of the largest companies in South Dakota are Citibank and John Morrell & Company. These companies are located in the Sioux Falls area. More than 10,000 people also work at Sioux Valley Hospital.

Tourism is the fastest-growing industry in the state. About eight million people visit South Dakota every year, spending $1.25 billion. More than 27,000 people work in tourism, running hotels and providing food and entertainment for visitors. While gambling casinos have brought some jobs to Native American reservations, the reservations are still among the poorest places in the United States. Few advances have been made to create more jobs in these rural areas.

A Native American woman sells handmade jewelry outside the entrance to Custer State Park.

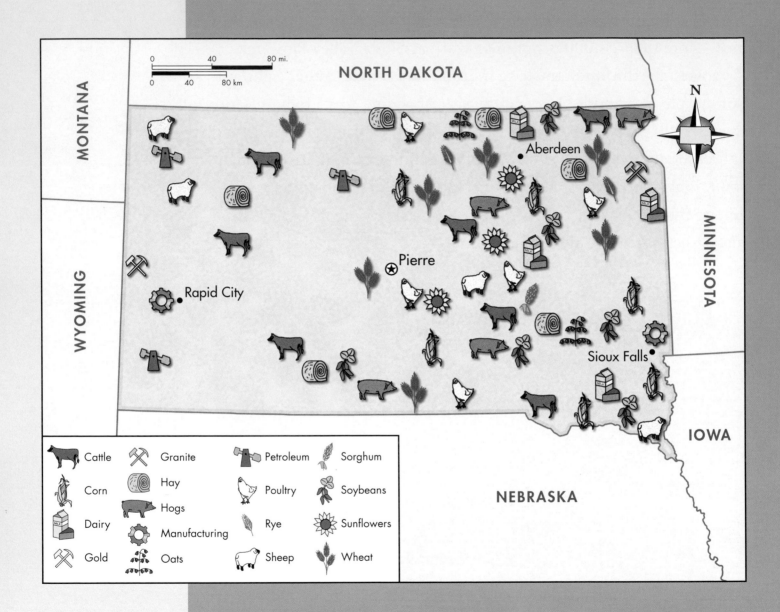

NORTH DAKOTA

MONTANA

WYOMING

MINNESOTA

IOWA

NEBRASKA

0   40   80 mi.
0   40   80 km

N

Aberdeen

Pierre

Rapid City

Sioux Falls

Icon	Label	Icon	Label	Icon	Label	Icon	Label
	Cattle		Granite		Petroleum		Sorghum
	Corn		Hay		Poultry		Soybeans
	Dairy		Hogs		Rye		Sunflowers
	Gold		Manufacturing		Sheep		Wheat
			Oats				

Eastern South Dakota

The first stop is Vermillion, in the southeastern foot of the state. A small town with about 10,000 residents, Vermillion is home to the University of South Dakota, which has America's Shrine to Music Museum on campus. It is a world-class museum with thousands of valuable musical instruments on display. There is even a 300-year-old violin made by Antonio Stradivari, the most famous violin maker in history.

Traveling north and east, you come to Sioux Falls, the largest city in South Dakota. The city grew up around the Big Sioux River 150 years ago. Today, Falls Park along the river is one of the city's most visited areas. Joggers enjoy the scenic beauty of the area as they run along the beautiful river walk. Take a ride on the Sioux Falls Trolley to explore other parts of the city, including the Outdoor Campus Museum. You can learn about the natural habitats of South Dakota there, including prairies, woodlands, and wetlands. You can also take classes to learn about fishing, outdoor skills, and even rock climbing.

Heading west through gently rolling farmland, you'll come to the small town of Mitchell, home of the world's only Corn Palace. Some people call the Corn Palace the world's largest birdfeeder, because every year 3,000 bushels of corncobs, grain, and grasses are used to create huge murals showing early life in South Dakota. The murals are changed every year. Inside are six beautiful murals by Oscar Howe, a famous Dakota artist. Long ago, famous bands played at the Corn

The Mitchell Corn Palace pays tribute to the agricultural heritage of South Dakota.

Palace, including John Philip Sousa. Basketball games are played there today.

Just outside of town is the Mitchell Prehistoric Indian Village, where you can see how people lived more than 1,000 years ago. It is the state's only National Archeological Landmark.

Driving along the fertile James River Valley, head north and then a bit east to the town of De Smet. If you've read any of the Laura Ingalls Wilder books, you will not want to miss this tiny town. De Smet is the real Little Town on the Prairie. Wilder lived in De Smet from the ages of twelve to twenty-seven. You can see the house that Pa built in 1887 and the house the family lived in before that, the surveyor's shanty.

At the Laura Ingalls Wilder Homestead, you can find out about life on the American frontier during the late 1800s.

Each summer, the town celebrates the Laura Ingalls Wilder Pageant. Scenes from the books are acted out, and there are free horse-drawn wagon rides for children.

It's a long way north, but the town of Aberdeen is worth a visit. L. Frank Baum, author of *The Wonderful Wizard of Oz*, lived there for a short time. Visit Storybook Land, see the Yellow Brick Road, and meet Dorothy, the Tin Man, the Cowardly Lion, and the Scarecrow.

West of Aberdeen is the quiet, friendly town of Mobridge. On a hill just outside of town you will find a 7-ton granite bust of Sitting Bull, the great Lakota chief. It was carved by Korczak Ziolkowski, who also carved the Crazy Horse Memorial. Sitting Bull was killed in 1890. In

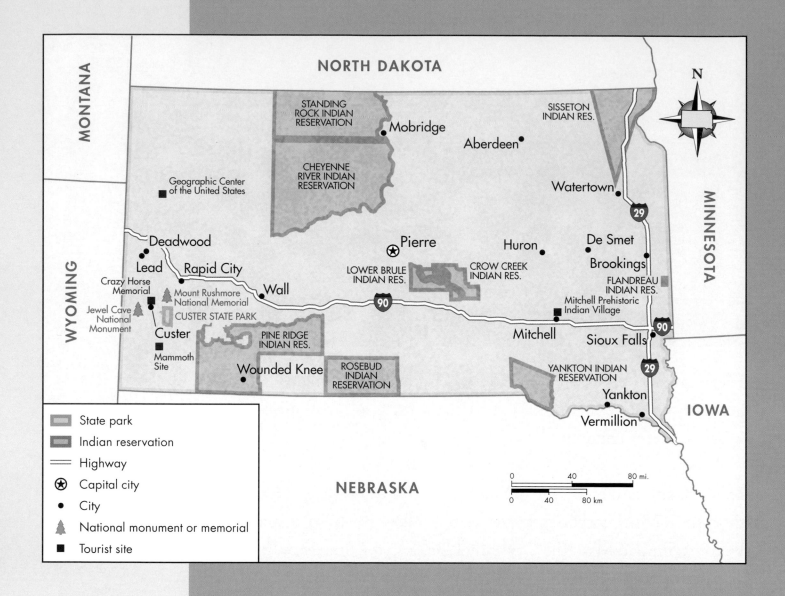

NORTH DAKOTA

MONTANA

STANDING ROCK INDIAN RESERVATION

SISSETON INDIAN RES.

Mobridge

Aberdeen

CHEYENNE RIVER INDIAN RESERVATION

Geographic Center of the United States

Watertown

MINNESOTA

29

Deadwood

WYOMING

Lead

Rapid City

Pierre

Huron

De Smet

Brookings

Crazy Horse Memorial

LOWER BRULE INDIAN RES.

CROW CREEK INDIAN RES.

Wall

90

FLANDREAU INDIAN RES.

Mount Rushmore National Memorial

Mitchell Prehistoric Indian Village

Jewel Cave National Monument

CUSTER STATE PARK

Custer

PINE RIDGE INDIAN RES.

Mitchell

Sioux Falls

90

Mammoth Site

YANKTON INDIAN RESERVATION

29

Wounded Knee

ROSEBUD INDIAN RESERVATION

Yankton

Vermillion

IOWA

NEBRASKA

State park

Indian reservation

Highway

⊛ Capital city

• City

🌲 National monument or memorial

■ Tourist site

0   40   80 mi.

0   40   80 km

N

1953 his descendants dug up his bones and reburied them there, near his birthplace.

Western South Dakota

Don't miss Wall Drug in the town of Wall. This is a popular stopping place for tourists and South Dakotans alike. All over South Dakota there are hundreds of billboards telling people to visit, so hop out and take a look for yourself.

From Wall, you can continue to one of the world's strangest and most mysterious places, the Badlands. Be sure to visit this area in the early morning or at sunset. These are the best times to see the colors in

Wall Drug has a unique collection of western items.

This skull of an oreodont was found in the Badlands of South Dakota.

The historic streets of Deadwood are filled with restaurants, entertainment, and a taste of the Wild West.

the rocks. Some people say the Badlands look like the surface of the moon. Wind and rain have carved deep canyons and jagged cliffs in the rock over the last 65 million years. The area is filled with fossils. If you're lucky enough to find one, do not remove it—these fossils are protected by law.

At Wounded Knee, you can see a memorial to the more than 300 Lakota Sioux massacred there on December 29, 1890. They were buried in a common grave. You can read some of the names aloud to honor them: Wolf Skin Necklace, No Ears, Bear Cuts Body, Spotted Thunder, and Big Skirt.

The Black Hills

The first stop in the Black Hills is the bustling town of Deadwood. Deadwood still feels like a Wild West town. Just like in old times, it is full of gamblers. Also be sure to visit Mount Moriah Cemetery, just outside town. You will see the graves of Wild Bill Hickok, Calamity Jane, Potato Creek Johnny, Preacher Smith, and others from gold rush times.

Speaking of the gold rush, the next stop is Lead (pronounced "leed," for a type of gravel). This town also sprouted up during the gold rush. The Homestake Gold Mine there was the oldest continuously operating gold mine in the world until it closed in 2001. Be sure to take the Homestake Mine Surface Tour and visit the Black Hills Mining Museum to learn the history and methods of mining.

Near Lead is Custer State Park, home to one of the state's largest buffalo herds. In 1889, when almost every buffalo in the United States had been killed, a man named Scotty Philip bought a tiny herd and began to breed buffalo. The herd grew to 900. Those buffalo are the ancestors of the ones you see at Custer State Park. Every September, Buffalo Round Up Day is celebrated there. All the buffalo are herded into corrals. Some are auctioned off, and the rest are returned to the park.

It is not unusual for herds of buffalo to stop traffic at Custer State Park.

Visitors to Mount Rushmore can enjoy a close-up view of the carvings as well as the visitor's center and museum.

The most famous place in South Dakota is Mount Rushmore, sometimes called the Shrine of Democracy. Try to visit in early morning when the sun lights up the 60-foot- (18-m-) high faces of Presidents George Washington, Thomas Jefferson, Theodore Roosevelt, and Abraham Lincoln. Gutzon Borglum, the sculptor who carved Mount Rushmore, worked on it from 1927 to 1941. He died just before it was completed, and his son finished the work.

Another unique sculpture is the Crazy Horse Memorial, north of Custer. It is the largest sculpture in the world. It pictures Crazy Horse on horseback pointing toward the Black Hills. The artist, Korczak Ziolkowski, assisted Borglum on the carving of Mount Rushmore. The idea for the Crazy Horse sculpture came from Chief Henry Standing Bear. Standing Bear once wrote to Ziolkowski saying the American Indians "would like the white man to know the red man has great

A model of the Crazy Horse Memorial is photographed in front of the work being carved.

heroes, too." The work began in 1948 and continues today. Since Ziolkowski's death in 1982, his wife and seven of his children have continued the work. When the entire sculpture is complete, it will be 563 feet (172 m) high and 642 feet (196 m) wide. The face alone is nine stories tall.

The next stop is the Mammoth Site, which has the remains of fifty-two prehistoric elephants called mammoths. This is the largest number uncovered anywhere in

Scientists still conduct research at Mammoth Site, where information about the past is uncovered through the study of fossils.

the world. Mammoths lived on grasslands about 26,000 years ago. There are also fossils of gray wolves, giant short-faced bears, and mink. Scientists left the bone and tusks where they were found so you can see for yourself how they were uncovered.

The Black Hills are filled with caves. The seventh largest cave in the world, Wind Cave, is there. You can see delicate crystal formations and wander along 81 miles (130 km) of passageways. Jewel Cave National Monument has formations that look like popcorn.

Finally, if you drive north, you can stand at the geographic center of the United States, including Alaska and Hawaii. It is off Route 85, 17 miles (27 km) west of Castle Rock in Butte County. It is exactly 44° 58' North, 103° 46' West. Have someone take your picture next to the marker.

Wind Cave is one of the world's longest and most complex caves.

SOUTH DAKOTA ALMANAC

Statehood date and number: November 2, 1889; 40th state

State seal: A gold circle with the words "State of South Dakota Great Seal" around an etching of the land showing a man plowing, a riverboat sailing upriver, a factory, and planted fields. Adopted in 1889.

State flag: The state seal surrounded by golden sun rays in a field of sky blue. Words around the seal read, "South Dakota, The Mount Rushmore State." Adopted in 1963; updated in 1992.

Geographic center: 100° 28.7' W, 44° 24.1' N; 8 miles (13 km) NE of Pierre

Total area/rank: 77,122 square miles (199,745 sq km)/17th

Borders: North Dakota, Minnesota, Iowa, Nebraska, Wyoming, and Montana

Latitude and longitude: South Dakota is located approximately between 45° 57' N and 43° N and 96° 26' and 104° 03' W

Highest/lowest elevation: Harney Peak, 7,242 feet (2,207 m)/Big Stone Lake, 962 feet (293 m)

Hottest/coldest temperature: 120° F (49° C) in Gann Valley on July 5, 1936/–58° F (–50° C) in McIntosh on February 17, 1936

Land area/rank: 75,896 square miles (196,571 sq km)/16th

Inland water area/rank: 1,225 square miles (3,173 sq km)/16th

Population/rank: 754,844 (2000)/46th

Population of major cities:

  Sioux Falls: 123,975

  Rapid City: 59,607

Origin of state name: *Dakota* is a Lakota word for "friends" or "allies."

State capital: Pierre

Counties: 66

State government: 35 senators, 70 representatives

Major rivers/lakes: Missouri, Big Sioux, Cheyenne, James, Vermilion, Grand, White, and Bad/Big Stone Lake, Lake Traverse, Oahe, Sharpe, Francis Case, Lewis and Clark

Farm products: Wheat, corn, oats, sunflowers, soybeans, sorghum, rye, flaxseed, hay

Livestock: Hogs, sheep, cattle

Manufactured products: Machinery, clothing, electronic equipment, food products

Mining products: Gold, silver, feldspar, mica, uranium, gravel

Animal: Coyote

Bird: Chinese ring-necked pheasant

Dessert: Kuchen

Drink: Milk

Fish: Walleye

Flower: American pasque flower

Fossil: Triceratops

Gemstone: Fairburn agate

Grass: Western wheat grass

Insect: Honey bee

Mineral: Rose quartz

Motto: "Under God the People Rule"

Musical instrument: Fiddle

Nicknames: Mount Rushmore State, Coyote State, Blizzard State, Sunshine State, Artesian State, Land of Infinite Variety

Soil: Houdek

Song: "Hail! South Dakota," words and music by DeeCort Hammitt; adopted in 1943

Tree: Black Hills spruce

Wildlife: Buffalo, bighorn sheep, Rocky Mountain goats, white-tailed deer, mule deer, elk, pronghorn deer, coyotes, beavers, minks, prairie dogs, prairie chickens, ducks, rattlesnakes, golden eagles, wild turkeys, sage grouses, Hungarian partridges, walleyed pikes, trout, northern pike, perch, bluegill, bass

TIME**LINE**

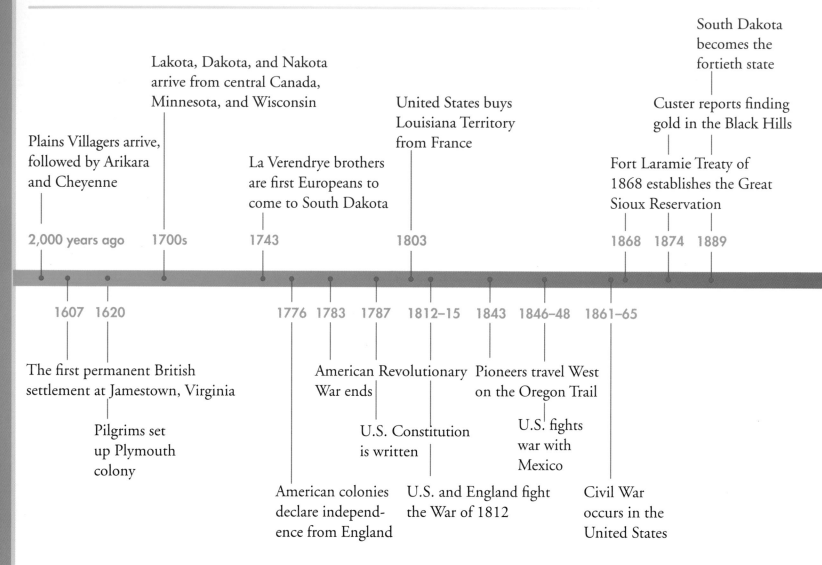

South Dakota becomes the fortieth state

Lakota, Dakota, and Nakota arrive from central Canada, Minnesota, and Wisconsin

United States buys Louisiana Territory from France

Custer reports finding gold in the Black Hills

Plains Villagers arrive, followed by Arikara and Cheyenne

La Verendrye brothers are first Europeans to come to South Dakota

Fort Laramie Treaty of 1868 establishes the Great Sioux Reservation

2,000 years ago | 1700s | 1743 | 1803 | 1868 | 1874 | 1889

1607 | 1620 | 1776 | 1783 | 1787 | 1812–15 | 1843 | 1846–48 | 1861–65

The first permanent British settlement at Jamestown, Virginia

American Revolutionary War ends

Pioneers travel West on the Oregon Trail

Pilgrims set up Plymouth colony

U.S. Constitution is written

U.S. fights war with Mexico

American colonies declare independence from England

U.S. and England fight the War of 1812

Civil War occurs in the United States

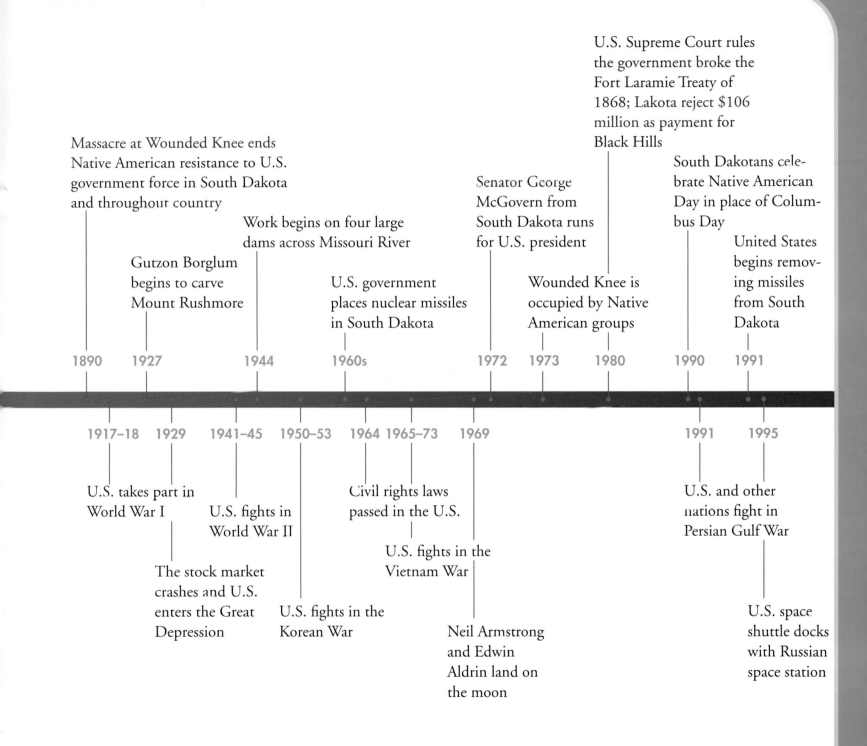

Massacre at Wounded Knee ends Native American resistance to U.S. government force in South Dakota and throughout country

Gutzon Borglum begins to carve Mount Rushmore

Work begins on four large dams across Missouri River

U.S. government places nuclear missiles in South Dakota

Senator George McGovern from South Dakota runs for U.S. president

U.S. Supreme Court rules the government broke the Fort Laramie Treaty of 1868; Lakota reject $106 million as payment for Black Hills

Wounded Knee is occupied by Native American groups

South Dakotans celebrate Native American Day in place of Columbus Day

United States begins removing missiles from South Dakota

1890   1927   1944   1960s   1972   1973   1980   1990   1991

1917–18   1929   1941–45   1950–53   1964   1965–73   1969   1991   1995

U.S. takes part in World War I

U.S. fights in World War II

Civil rights laws passed in the U.S.

U.S. and other nations fight in Persian Gulf War

The stock market crashes and U.S. enters the Great Depression

U.S. fights in the Vietnam War

U.S. fights in the Korean War

Neil Armstrong and Edwin Aldrin land on the moon

U.S. space shuttle docks with Russian space station

GALLERY OF FAMOUS SOUTH DAKOTANS

Sparky Anderson

(1934–)

First baseball manager to manage World Series winners in both the American League and the National League. He was the manager of the Detroit Tigers and the Cincinnati Reds. Lived in Bridgewater.

Tom Brokaw

(1940–)

Nationally known news commentator. Born in Webster.

Tom Daschle

(1947–)

Leader of the Democratic Party in the United States Senate. He is known for having strong opinions and for encouraging people to work together to solve problems. Born in Aberdeen.

Oscar Howe

(1915–1983)

Dakota artist whose colorful paintings are well known in South Dakota and around the world. He painted scenes from Indian life. In 1960, Howe was named artist laureate of South Dakota, meaning he was the finest artist in the state. Born on the Crow Creek Reservation.

Hubert H. Humphrey

(1911–1978)

Thirty-eighth vice president of the United States. Humphrey worked hard for civil rights. Born in Wallace.

George McGovern

(1922–)

United States senator for three terms, beginning in 1962. In 1972, McGovern ran for president of the United States on the Democratic ticket. Born in Avon.

Billy Mills

(1938–)

Won a gold medal at the 1964 Olympics for the 10,000-meter track race. In 1965, Mills set the world record for the 6-mile run. Grew up on the Pine Ridge Reservation.

Mary Pyle

(1866–1949)

Fought for women's suffrage, or the right to vote. Because of her efforts, South Dakota granted women the right to vote in state elections in 1918. Lived in Miller, Dakota Territory.

Casey Tibbs

(1929–1990)

Rodeo cowboy. He won twenty-one world championships and was elected to the World Cowboy Hall of Fame. Born in Fort Pierre.

GLOSSARY

amend: to change or revise

bison: proper term for the American buffalo

blizzard: freezing, windy snowstorm

bust: a sculpture showing a person's head, neck, and part of the shoulders and chest

butte: flat-topped, rocky hill that stands alone

capital: city where the government meets

capitol: the building in which state lawmakers meet

chinook: fast-moving, warm wind that can cause rapid temperature changes

condense: to change gas or vapor into liquid form

drought: period of time in which little or no rain falls

fossil: the remains, or an impression left by them, of a plant or animal from long ago preserved in the Earth's crust

homestead: to settle land and farm it, especially under the Homestead Act

hydroelectric: the production of electricity by water power

initiative: a proposed law suggested by citizens, without the legislature

loam: a loose, rich soil of clay and sand

mural: artwork made directly on a wall

plains: very dry, rolling or flat grasslands

prairie: grasslands

reservation: land where Native Americans live and govern themselves

soddie: nickname for a sod house, which is made of soil that is cut and stacked like bricks

tourism: the business of providing food, shelter, and entertainment for visitors

treaty: a formal, signed agreement

veto: the right to refuse or reject something

FOR MORE INFORMATION

Web sites

State of South Dakota Web Site

http://www.state.sd.us
News about South Dakota, as well as links to information about government and travel.

The Weekly South Dakotan

http://www.sd4history.com
Excellent site for students covering South Dakota history and people.

South Dakota State Library

http://www.sdstatelibrary.com/forkids/southdakota.htm
Links to information about famous places, people, and Native American tribes.

Students' Section of Governor's Office of Economic Development

http://www.sdgreatprofits.com/SC.htm
Contains charts with information about the people of South Dakota as well as information about the state's history and symbols.

Books

Anderson, William. *Laura Ingalls Wilder Country*. New York: Harper Perennial, 1990.

Blumberg, Rhoda. *The Incredible Journey of Lewis and Clark*. New York: Lothrop, Lee & Shepard, 1987.

Freedman, Russell. *Buffalo Hunt*. New York: Holiday House, 1998.

Santella, Andrew. *Mount Rushmore*. Danbury, CT: Children's Press, 1999.

Santella, Andrew. *The Lakota Sioux*. Danbury, CT: Children's Press, 2001.

Addresses

Governor of South Dakota

500 East Capitol Avenue
Pierre, SD 57501

South Dakota State Historical Society

900 Governors Drive
Pierre, SD 57501

South Dakota Chamber of Congress and Industry

P. O. Box 190
Pierre, SD 57501

INDEX

ABOUT THE AUTHOR

Caryn Yacowitz grew up in Ohio and New Jersey, where she learned about Native Americans from her father. When she was a child, she hunted for arrowheads everywhere. She likes to travel to famous and out-of-the-way places and talk to all kinds of people. Yacowitz has written several picture books and a series of books about Native American tribes.